SCOOBY-DOO!

MONSTER JOKE BOOK

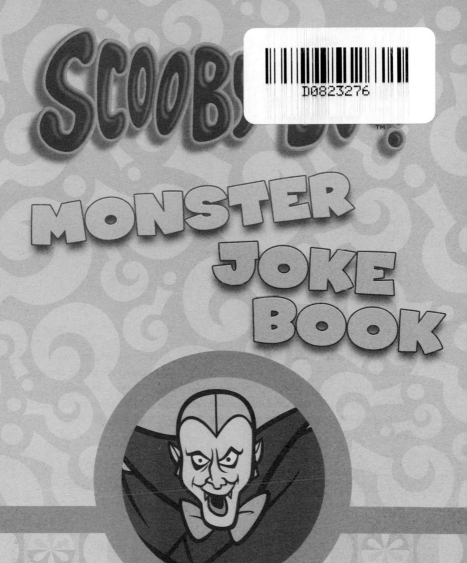

By Howie Dewin

SCHOLASTIC INC.
New York Toronto London Auckland Sydney
Mexico City New Delhi Hong Kong

No part of this publication may be reproduced in whole or in part, or stored
in a retrieval system, or transmitted in any form or by any means, electronic, mechanical, photocopying, recording, or otherwise, without written permission
of the publisher. For information regarding permission, write to Scholastic Inc.,
Attention: Permissions Department, 557 Broadway, New York, NY 10012.

ISBN 978-0-545-37944-1

Copyright © 2011 Hanna-Barbera. SCOOBY-DOO and all related characters
and elements are trademarks of and © Hanna-Barbera.

Used under license by Scholastic Inc. All rights reserved.
Published by Scholastic Inc. SCHOLASTIC and associated logos are trademarks
and/or registered trademarks of Scholastic Inc.

12 11 10 9 8 7 6 5 4 3 2 1   11 12 13 14 15 16/0

Cover design by Kay Petronio
Interior design by Bethany Dixon
Printed in the U.S.A.   40
This edition, September 2011

Hey there, mystery fans!

Greetings from the Coolsonian Criminology Museum, the grooviest museum ever built. It's jam-packed with amazing stuff from Coolsville's hottest detectives' (that's us!) biggest cases. You'll see displays of the scariest costumes we've ever pulled off a bad guy (or girl).

But don't be afraid! Take the tour with us. We're so brave we can make jokes about anything. That's how it is when you're really, really cooooool.

So keep your eye out for the Black Knight Ghost, Redbeard's Ghost, the Creeper, the Ozark Witch, and the Cotton Candy Glob. Yikes! It's getting scary just talking about it. Time for some jokes!

Yours in yuks,

Fred

Velma

Scooby

Shaggy

Daphne

Scientific Name
Mysteromous Coolisis

Common Name
Meet Coolsville's Coolest Kids

Fred here — the good-looking, athletic, fearless brains behind Mystery, Inc. Here are a few groovy jokes for you!

Why are athletes so cool?
Because they're always surrounded by fans!

What's a sprinter's favorite drink?
Running water.

If athletes get athlete's foot, what do astronauts get?
Missile toe!

Being cool, brave, and good-looking can be tough. It's lonely at the top.

What did the Astroturf say to the football field? Don't move! I gotcha covered!

Knock-knock.
Who's there?
Handsome.
Handsome who?
Hand some of that pizza to me!

Velma: Hey Fred, why are you folding your dollar bills in half?
Fred: I want to double my money!

How many Freds would it take to change a lightbulb?
None. Fred's so brave he doesn't mind the dark.

I think it's fair to say that I, Velma, am the true brains behind Mystery, Inc., although I don't like to show off!

What kind of math has to do with gardening?
Gee-I'm-a-Tree

What's the best tool to bring to math class?
Multi-pliers.

How many feet are in a yard?
Depends on how many people are standing in it!

What was Daphne's favorite subject in school?
Buy-ology!

I'd like to state, for the record, that it's scientifically impossible for us to be totally **HOT** and totally **COOL** at the same time — no matter what Fred says.

Why shouldn't you do math around cannibals?
Because if you add 4 and 4, you get 8.

What did Shaggy's teachers used to yell at him for NOT doing?
His homework!

Which classes didn't Fred fail?
The ones he didn't take!

What do you call a really groovy beaded watchband?
Accessory to the time.

All I know is that I'm Daphne — I may not always have the answers, but I know what looks good with any outfit!

Why did the vampire fall in love with Daphne?
He said she reminded him of the girl necks door.

What did Daphne name her fierce, fire-eating kitty?
Fluffy the Campfire Slayer!

What magazine do chipmunks read?
Cover Squirrel.

> Girls just want to have fun . . . and solve the hardest mysteries, and look good while they're doing it.

Why did Daphne use a shampoo with bullets?
She wanted her hair to have bangs.

Where do ace detectives like us get our groceries?
The snooper market.

How did we finally conquer the Giant Hamburger Monster?
We grilled the suspect!

Knock knock.
Who's there?
Men.
Men who?
No, thanks. Just give me the fries!

What did Shaggy yell when he hid beneath his covers?
I'm not scared, I'm just going undercover!

What does Scooby like to drink when he's washing down a Scooby Snack?
Dr. Pupper.

What looks exactly like Shaggy, but weighs nothing?
His shadow!

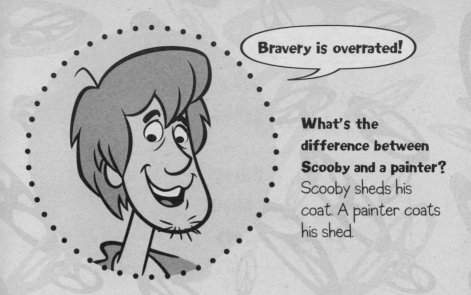

Bravery is overrated!

What's the difference between Scooby and a painter? Scooby sheds his coat. A painter coats his shed.

What did the witch doctor say to Daphne? Voodoo like to dance?

Who does a mummy take on a date? Anyone he can dig up.

What's a vampire's favorite tree? A ceme-tree.

Zoinks!

Scientific Name
Goodus vs. Badus

Common Name
Good Jokes About
Bad Monsters

Shaggy: I'm
a teepee!
I'm a wigwam!
I'm a teepee!
I'm a wigwam!
Velma: Relax!
You're two tents!
Shaggy: Like,
I can't help it!
We're surrounded by bad guys!

**What's the best way to keep the 10,000 Volt Ghost
from striking?**
Pay him a good salary!

**What's Scooby's idea of the best way to talk to
a monster?**
From a long, long way away!

**What did the
monster's mother say
when her daughter got older?**
She's certainly gruesome!

Best-Selling Bad Guy Books

The Mummy's Handbook by I.B.N. Rapt

My Life as a Vampire by Drew Blood

The Werewolf's Confession by Rip U. Tashreds

A Monster's Job by Bea Vishus

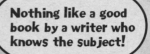

Nothing like a good book by a writer who knows the subject!

Best-Selling Good Guy Books

Why I Became a Private Eye by Wanda Findum

The Endless Search for Evil by Sarah Vilinere

How to Catch a Bad Guy by Kip Luhkin

True Tales of Terror by Dun Chasingools

Daphne: Did you hear about the monster who ate a whole family?
Velma: That's a little tough to swallow.

How do you handle a blue monster?
Tell him a joke to cheer him up!

What do you call one hundred acres filled with monsters?
A terror-tory.

What did the vampire do when his shift at work was half over?
He took a coffin break.

Zoinks! These jokes are scarier than the monsters!

What's the Ghost of Redbeard's favorite meal?
Fish and ships.

How much does Redbeard's Ghost pay to have his ears pierced?
A buck-an-ear!

How did the bad guy keep Scooby from barking?
He gave him hush puppies.

When did the detective find out the villain was in the belfry?
When the bell tolled.

What did the ghost of Farmer Brown call his cows with two legs?
Lean beef.

What did the ghost of Farmer Brown call his cows with no legs?
Ground beef.

You can say that again!

Why did the Spirit of the Black Knight stop asking Daphne out on dates?
He knew he didn't stand a ghost of a chance.

19

Scientific Name
Monstertorium

Common Name
Creepy Creature
Crack-Ups

Q: One cannibal asked another cannibal how long people should be cooked. What did the second cannibal say?
A: "Same as short ones."

Like, don't make jokes about things that go bump in the night. They might hear you!

How did the cannibal congratulate his friend?
He toasted him.

What did the cannibal say to her son when he chased the mailman?
Stop playing with your food.

Did you hear about the cannibal lion?
He had to swallow his pride!

Where do slimy, oozing, one-eyed monsters shop?
The gross-ery store.

What's the best way to keep a stinky monster from smelling?
Plug his nose!

What did the Giant Slug Monster shout when its victim escaped?
I'll get you next slime!

What did one zombie say to another?
Get a life!

Why did the Cyclops have to shut down his school?
Because he only had one pupil.

What did the monster couple like to do after dinner?
Go out for an evening troll.

Where do baby ghouls go during the day?
Day scare.

What do you call two witches who live together?
Broommates.

Daphne: What kind of horse should you ride at night?
Scooby: Reats re!
Daphne: A night-mare!

Why did the one-handed monster cross the road?
To get to the sec-ondhand shop.

What did the werewolf say when he left his victim?
Nice gnawin' you.

What does Scooby call a deserted town full of great food?
A roast town.

Why did Shaggy confuse a mummy and the packages under his Christmas tree?
One was a wrapped presence and the others were wrapped presents!

Why was Scooby afraid to go to the shoe store?
He was afraid of all the soles!

Why couldn't Scooby and Shaggy find their way out of the ghost town?
They kept coming to dead ends.

Daphne: Yikes! Frog Man has been here!
Fred: How do you know?
Daphne: There's an empty Croaka-Cola bottle!

What do you call a little girl ghoul who climbs trees and runs wild?
A tomb-boy.

What did the zombie say when he buried the detective?
You're in deep trouble now!

Why did the skeleton cross the road?
To get to the body shop.

What do skeletons say before they eat?
Bone appétit!

Why wouldn't the skeleton cross the road?
He had no guts!

I've got a bone to pick with whoever's making up these jokes!

What did one skeleton say to another when they met on the street?
Bonejour.

What did the extraterrestrial skeleton want to do?
Bone home.

What do you call a skeleton who can't carry a tune?
Bone-deaf.

Why did the idiot monster shoot his bowl of bran flakes?
He wanted to be a cereal killer.

Scientific Name
Villainous Stupidiferous

Common Name
Big Bad Buffoons!

Why did the pitcher wear a face mask when his team played the witches?
He heard their bats really flew!

Why wouldn't the vampire eat an orange?
He preferred neck-tarines.

What happened to the nitwit who didn't pay the exorcist?
He was repossessed.

Why did Big Bad Bald Bill paint rabbits on his head?
From a distance, they looked like hares.

Rupid ris ras rupid roes!

Why did the numskull ghost stay out of the wildlife preserve?
He heard he needed a haunting license.

Why did the werewolf go to New York City?
He wanted to visit the Vampire State Building.

Why did the doctor prescribe cold medicine for the vampire?
He said his coffin put him flat on his back!

Why did the Headless Horseman open a savings account?
He wanted to get a head.

Why did the mummy refuse to go on vacation?
He didn't want to unwind.

Why did the stupid vampire take the top off his coffin?
He was tired of things going over his head.

Velma: Did you hear about the ship that was so loaded down with vampires that it sank?
Shaggy: Now that's what I call a blood vessel!

Why did the goblin's wife stop ordering dessert?
She was trying to keep her ghoulish figure.

Why did the mummy avoid a life of crime?
He was afraid of being strip-searched!

Knock knock.
Who's there?
Juan.
Juan who?
Juan monster!

Knock knock.
Who's there?
Ann.
Ann who?
Ann-other monster!

Knock knock.
Who's there?
Moira.
Moira who?
Moira monsters!

Knock knock.
Who's there?
Evan.
Evan who?
Evan MORE monsters!

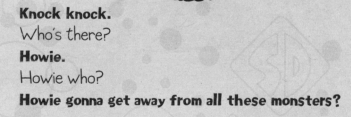

Knock knock.
Who's there?
Howie.
Howie who?
Howie gonna get away from all these monsters?

Shaggy: Knock knock.
Scooby: Rho's rhere?
Shaggy: A troll. He's too short to ring the doorbell.

Nurse: Doctor, there's a ghost here to meet you.
Doctor: Tell her I can't see her.

What do you call a really stupid monster who makes nice sweaters?
A knit wit.

Why couldn't the Ghost of Redbeard play cards while pirates were on his ship?
Because they were standing on the deck.

Ruh-roh! Rore rupid rokes!

Why did the werewolf take so many baths?
He wanted to be a wash-and-werewolf.

What's white, has a wand, and gives money to young vampires?
The Fang Fairy.

Why did the Abominable Snowman paint his toenails red?
So he could hide in the strawberry patch.

Scientific Name
Screaminous Meaminous

Common Name
Yikes 'n' Yuks!

Which monster can you only find in the forest?
Frankenpine.

Which monster can you only find in a cave?
Frankenmine.

Which monster is always at a restaurant?
Frankendine.

Which monster loves to garden?
Frankenvine.

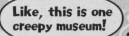

Like, this is one creepy museum!

Which monster gave up telling bad jokes?
Frankenresign.

Which monster is always complaining?
Frankenwhine.

What do ghosts do to keep safe when they're driving?
They boo-kle their safety belts.

Where do mummies like to go on vacation?
The Dead Sea.

Where do goblins go to buy stamps?
The ghost office.

What do little girl monsters sell door-to-door?
Ghoul Scout Cookies.

What did Dr. Frankenstein say as he put the finishing touches on his new monster creation?
Let's bolt!

Velma: What could possibly be scarier than being asked out on a date?
Daphne: Not being asked?

Which ghoul won the title of Miss Skeleton?
No body.

How does a witch keep her hair looking just right?
Scarespray.

What's the cannibal monster's favorite game?
Swallow the leader!

What does the Abominable Snowman eat after he tramples a village?
Squash.

What does a ghost read in the morning?
The boospaper.

What are the two things a cannibal can't eat for breakfast?
Lunch and dinner.

How do you keep a giant monster from charging?
Take away its credit cards.

Fred: What should you do if you find a bloodthirsty monster in your bed?
Velma: Sleep somewhere else.

How did the newspapers describe the winner of the Miss Monster beauty contest?
"Pretty Ugly!"

What's the worst day of the week to meet a cannibal?
Chewsday.

Why did the cannibal lose his job?
He was buttering up the boss.

What happened to the actors who tried to perform in the haunted theater?

They got a bad case of stage fright.

What did the phantom email his phantom friend after he'd moved out of town?

You are mist.

Shaggy: Imagine you're trapped in a haunted house filled with vampires and cannibals. How do you survive?
Velma: Stop imagining.

How do vampires celebrate their blessings?
Fangsgiving.

What did the fire-breathing alien say just before he attacked?
Nice to heat you!

Scientific Name
Galactic & Extinctus
Monsteromous

Common Name
Far-Out Funnies!

Where do aliens leave their spacecrafts?
At parking meteors.

What's an alien's favorite key on the computer?
The space bar.

UFO? Everybody knows what that means, dude! Unidentified Freaky Object!

How do space monsters throw a party?
They planet.

How do space monsters get a baby to fall asleep?
They rocket.

What happened when the fruit bat monster was put on trial?
He was convicted by a jury of his pears.

What's a big, bad dinosaur monster's favorite number?
8

How did Velma feel after she was attacked by the prehistoric monster?
Dino-SORE!

What did Shaggy say after the gang finished fighting the dinosaur's ghost?
Tyrannosaurus wrecks!

What's the scariest of the dinosaur monsters?
The Terror-dactyl!

Talk about old jokes!

Why did the factory workers run when the vegetarian dinosaur headed toward their building?
Because everyone knows that vegetarians are PLANT eaters!

What kind of spell did the wizard put on the dinosaur?
A Tyrannosaurus hex.

What did the mother buffalo monster say to her son when he left for school?
Bison!

How do monsters predict their futures?
They read their horror-scopes.

Why do skeletons stay so calm?
Nothing gets under their skin.

Do monsters eat chicken with their fingers?
No. They eat fingers for dessert.

Fred: Why did the ghost wear sunglasses?
Daphne: I don't know. Why?
Fred: He thought they made him look ghoul.

**What do you call a vampire
who falls for practical jokes?**
A real sucker!

**What did Velma say
to the ancient, smelly
swamp monster?**
You extinct!

What kind of music did the mummy like best?

Ragtime!

What did the cannibal order at the fast-food restaurant?
A handburger.

What do you call a skeleton that refuses to work?
Lazy bones!

Where did the phantom go to pick up his mail?
The dead letter office.

Why are ghost gatherings so boring?
There's no one to be the life of the party!

Scientific Name
Problemus & Solutionus

Common Name
**Crime-Solving
Knee Slappers!**

**What did Sherlock Holmes use
to piece his cases together?**
Crazy Clue.

**Why was Dr. Frankenstein
depressed?**
He'd just broken up with his
ghoulfriend.

**How did the mad scientist invent
bug spray?**
From scratch.

Daphne: Knock-knock.
Fred: Who's there?
Daphne: Police.
Fred: Police who?
Daphne: Police stop these terrible jokes!

How does Velma's favorite bedtime story begin?
Once upon a crime . . .

What did the detective say when his boss asked him about the search for the Giant Insect Monster?
I'm looking for the ant-sir!

What did E.T. say when he needed a detective to find his missing spaceship?
Phone Holmes.

What do you get when you cross a great detective with a ghost?
Sherlock Moans.

What do you get when you cross a great detective with a skeleton?
Sherlock Bones.

What do you get when you cross a great detective with a bad comedian?
Sherlock Groans.

These jokes are a crime!

What do you get when you cross a great detective with a banker?
Sherlock Loans.

What do you get when you cross a great detective with an ice cream truck?
Sherlock Cones.

How did Count Dracula write his life story?
In blood type.

How did Dracula describe his date with the pretty robot?
Love at first byte!

Why did Dracula punish his son?
He was acting like a spoiled bat.

What does Dracula drink to wake up?
Coffinated beverages.

Shaggy: What do little vampire detectives learn in kindergarten?
Scooby: Ri ron't rhow. Rhat?
Shaggy: The alphabat!

How did the mad scientist transform the train conductor into a monster cannibal?
He hypnotized him, and then told him to listen to his train — choo-choo-choo.

Why did the monster take a bath after eating all his victims?
He wanted to make a clean getaway.

What was Velma's favorite game when she was little?
Corpse and robbers.

What did the detective tell his neighbors when he left town in search of a witch?
I'm going away for a spell.

Jinkies! That's spooky!

What book was written by a guy who was attacked by a werewolf?
How to Survive a Monster Attack by I.M. Fien

Why do detectives have such a hard time catching ghosts?
It's tough to pin anything on them.

What did the star of the blockbuster vampire movie do when he became a big star?
He started a fang club.

Scientific Name
Coolsville Superstarus

Common Name
Hollywood Hysteria!

What did one Hollywood witch say to another?
Let's make movie magic!

Where does the skeleton starlet spend her days off?
In bed eating bonebones.

Why are there so many movie-star werewolves?
They like living in Howllywood.

Making a movie is not all fun and games . . . a lot of it is hair and makeup!

What kind of ice cream did the movie-star vampire have in his dressing room?
Veinilla.

How did the mad scientist become such a famous comedian?
He had a way of leaving people in stitches.

Why did the skeleton think he was going to get the starring role in the monster movie?
He could feel it in his bones.

What did the director of *The Monster Lumberjack* have to learn NOT to say while they were shooting the movie?
Ax-tion! And CUT!

Where did the mummy actor like to stand when he was on stage?
Dead center.

Why did the mummy get hired to stand in for the movie star?
He was a dead ringer.

How did the director address his monster star?
Very politely.

What movie was Count Dracula the star of?
The Vampire Strikes Back.

Show business is my laugh — I mean, life!

Which movie starred a bunch of monster dolls?
Toy Gory.

What movie's superhero got run over by a wild bunch of giant monsters?

Flatman.

Just remember —

when it comes to defending yourself against monsters, there's nothing scarier than a bad joke.

SCOOBY-DOO!

A to Z ULTIMATE JOKE BOOK

By Howie Dewin & MJ Barba

SCHOLASTIC INC.
New York Toronto London Auckland Sydney
Mexico City New Delhi Hong Kong

No part of this publication may be reproduced in whole or in part, stored in a
retrieval system, or transmitted in any form or by any means, electronic, mechanical,
photocopying, recording, or otherwise, without written permission of the publisher.
For information regarding permission, write to Scholastic Inc., Attention: Permissions
Department, 557 Broadway, New York, NY 10012.

ISBN 978-0-545-37944-1

Copyright © 2011 Hanna-Barbera. SCOOBY-DOO and all related characters and
elements are trademarks of and © Hanna-Barbera.

Used under license by Scholastic Inc. All rights reserved.
Published by Scholastic Inc. SCHOLASTIC and associated logos are trademarks
and/or registered trademarks of Scholastic Inc.

12 11 10 9 8 7 6 5 4 3 2 1   11 12 13 14 15/0

Designed by Kay Petronio
Printed in the U.S.A.   40
First printing, September 2011

Hey there, mystery lovers!

Thanks for flipping this book over! This is our A to Z joke book. Here you'll find some of our favorite jokes ever — from alien gags to cracks that are so strange they'll make you say ZOINKS! And this is the best part: These jokes won't scare you like the creepy monster punch lines on the other end of this book.

Now, we're not saying there are NO monsters, skeletons, and ghouls running in this direction — so keep your eyes peeled. But we can guarantee you'll crack up over a whole lot more than monsters once you crack this side of the book!

So, turn the page and start joking around!

Over 200 Monsters Defeated

Scooby   Shaggy   Velma   Daphne   Fred

A
ALIENS &
OUTER SPACE

What's an alien's favorite candy?
Martian-mallows.

Why did the star go to the bathroom?
It had to twinkle.

What do space cows say?
"Mooooo-n."

What is an alien's favorite sport?
Spaceball!

Why did the astronaut wear a clown suit?
He wanted a loonier landing.

What do you get when you cross an alien with a crybaby?
An unidentified crying object!

ARCHEOLOGY

What do you call a dinosaur in a cowboy hat and boots?
Tyrannosaurus Tex.

Why did the dinosaur cross the road?
Because chickens weren't invented yet.

What is an archeologist?
Someone whose career is in ruins!

B

BURGERS & SHAKES

How do they serve burgers in Transylvania?
Very rare-ly.

What did the judge say to the hamburger?
"Grill-ty as charred!"

Why did Shaggy toss Scooby a veggie burger?
He wanted to throw him a surprise patty!

What do cows use to prevent crimes?
Burger alarms!

POP

How do witches like their burgers?
Medium-scared!

What do burgers and high school kids have in common?
They're both pro-teen!

How do you make a milk shake?
Give it a good scare!

C
CLOWNS

**Why did the lion spit
out the clown?**
Because he tasted
funny!

**Which clown has
the biggest shoes?**
The one with the
biggest feet!

**Why did the clown
wear loud socks?**
So his feet wouldn't
fall asleep!

COWS

What's a steer's favorite holiday?
Moo-year's Day!

What do you call a cow who can't give milk?
An udder failure.

What do you get from a pampered cow?
Spoiled milk.

Why are cowboys bad at math?
They always round things up.

What do cows like about school?
Field trips.

D
DAPHNE'S FAVORITES

**What did Daphne say when
her teacher asked her to
use the word "fascinate"
in a sentence?**
"If I had a sweater with ten
buttons and two fell off, then
I would only have to fasten-
eight!"

**Why did Daphne put lipstick
on her forehead?**
She was trying to makeup her mind.

**Where did the fortune teller
go on vacation?**
To Palm Beach.

 10

Why did the writer visit the cemetery?
He needed a good plot.

Why did the thief want to be in the school musical?
So he could steal the show.

What type of music do balloons hate?
Pop music!

What did Daphne say when she ordered her school photos?
"Someday my prints will come."

DESERT ISLANDS

What do you call a cute volcano?
Lava-ble.

What kind of bus crossed the ocean?
Christopher ColumBUS.

**What did the Atlantic Ocean say to
the Pacific Ocean?**
Nothing, they just waved.

DOGS & CATS

Why does Scooby get hot in the summer?
Because he has a coat and pants.

What happened when the cat ate the ball of yarn?
It had mittens.

Where do you find a no-legged dog?
Right where you left him.

What kind of exam do you give Scooby?
A pup quiz!

EASY ANSWERS

(These are jokes even Shaggy can get!)

Why did 6 hate 7?
7 8 9.

What did the glue say to the teacher?
"I'm stuck on you."

Where did the pencil go for vacation?
To Pennsylvania.

ENCHANTMENTS & OTHER SPELLS

What kind of coffee do wizards prefer?
Maxspell House.

Where did the magician like to surf?
In the Pacific Potion.

Why is it hard to stop staring at a witch's book of magic?
Because the way it's put together is spell-binding.

What do you send a witch at camp?
A scare package.

Why do magicians make good teachers?
They ask trick questions.

F

FRED'S FAVORITES

What's a ghost's favorite soccer position?
Ghoul keeper.

Teacher: Where is the Dead Sea?
Fred: Wow. I didn't even know it was sick!

16

**What kind of illness
does a karate master
get?**
Kung Flu!

**What did the tree
wear to the pool
party?**
Swimming trunks!

How do boney folks start their cars?
Skeleton keys!

What do you get when burglars go surfing?
A crime wave.

Knock Knock.
Who's there?
Soccer.
Soccer who?
Soccer in the arm so she won't knock!

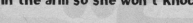

FARM FOLKS

What do you call a pig that does karate?
A pork chop.

What do you call a sleeping bull?
A bulldozer!

What has four legs and flies?
A pig!

How did the farmer count his cows?
On a cow-culator.

What did the horse get on his test?
Hay plus.

FUNNY & FURRY

What's a rabbit's favorite kind of music?
Hip-hop!

How do you know when a rabbit is exhausted?
He runs out of bounds.

What did the judge say when the skunk arrived in the courtroom?
"Odor in the court!"

GHOSTS & GRAVEYARDS

What does a baby ghost need at a restaurant?
A BOOster seat!

How do you erase a ghost?
White out!

What did the mommy ghost say to the baby ghost as they got into the car?
"Put on your sheet belt!"

Why are graveyards so noisy?
Because there's so much coffin.

When can't you bury people in the graveyard?
When they're not dead!

What runs around a cemetery but doesn't move?
A fence!

What do you call mother and father ghosts?
Transparents!

H

HAUNTED HOUSES & GHOULISH GHOULS

What did Dracula say when he was finished?
"BATS all, folks!"

What do you call a witch in the desert?
A sandwich!

What's a zombie's favorite Shakespeare play?
Romeo and Ghouliet.

Why did the ghoul get an answering machine?
He likes to scream his calls.

What time is it when Fred, Daphne, Velma, Shaggy, and Scooby chase a ghoul?
Five after one!

Why doesn't Dracula have more friends?
He's a pain in the neck!

HOLIDAYS

Who's never hungry at Thanksgiving?
The turkey. He's already stuffed!

How many Easter eggs can you fit into an empty basket?
One. After that, it's not empty!

IMAGINARY FRIENDS & INVISIBLE PEOPLE

What did Shaggy's imaginary friend say when Shaggy asked if he wanted to play school?
"Okay. But I'm absent."

Why did Scooby get rid of his pencil-headed imaginary friend?
Because he couldn't see the point.

What steps should you take if a double-headed, ten-foot tall imaginary friend comes rushing at you?
Great big ones.

When it comes to imaginary friends, two's company and three's a crowd. What is four and five?
Nine.

What's the difference between an American imaginary friend and a French imaginary friend?
About 3,000 or 4,000 miles.

How does Shaggy know he's having a bad day?
His imaginary friend won't play with him.

What's the worst thing to say to an imaginary friend?
"Long time, no see!"

JACK-O-LANTERNS

What did one jack-o-lantern say to the other?
"Cut it out!"

Why do jack-o-lanterns have stupid smiles on their faces?
You'd have a stupid smile, too, if you'd just had all your brains scooped out!

How do you repair a broken jack-o-lantern?
Buy a pumpkin patch!

What's black, white, orange, and waddles?
A penguin carrying a jack-o-lantern.

What's Velma's favorite desert?
Pumpkin pi.

JETS, PLANES & OTHER FLYING THINGS

How far can a remote-control plane fly after a wing falls off?
All the way to the crash site!

What do you call a peanut in a space capsule?
An astro-nut!

Knock Knock.
Who's There?
Plane.
Plane who?
Plane dumb won't fool me! I know you know who I am!

K KNOCK KNOCKS

Knock Knock.
Who's there!
Burglar!
Burglar who?
Burglars don't knock!

Knock Knock.
Who's there?
Catch.
Catch who?
Bless you!

Knock Knock.
Who's there?
Hawaii.
Hawaii who?
I'm fine, Hawaii you?

Knock Knock.
Who's there?
Cows.
Cows who?
No they don't, they moo!

Knock Knock.
Who's there?
Little old lady.
Little old lady who?
I didn't know you could yodel!

Knock Knock.
Who's there?
Dwayne.
Dwayne who?
Dwayne the tub! I'm dwoning!

L
LITTLE TINY THINGS

Knock Knock.
Who's there?
Mice Eyes.
Mice Eyes who?
My size is Extra Small!

What washes up on very small beaches?
Microwaves!

What medicine would you give a sick ant?
Antibiotics!

LOST & FOUND

Why is a lost Dalmatian easily found?
Because he's always spotted.

Why did the zombie go crazy?
Because he lost his mind!

Why couldn't the tennis player start a fire?
She lost all her matches.

Why was the broom absent?
It overswept.

M
MEDICAL ADVICE

What did the doctor say to the shrinking man?
"You'll just have to be a little patient."

What did one tonsil say to the other tonsil?
"Get dressed up, the doctor is taking us out!"

Why did the pillow go to the doctor?
He was feeling all stuffed up!

MYSTERY, INC.

Fred: You should never tell secrets on a farm.
Shaggy: Why?
Fred: Because the potatoes have eyes and the corn have ears!

Scooby: Rhat ro rou rall ra rentist rho's rin rhe rarmy?
Shaggy: A drill sergeant!

What kind of vegetable do you get when Scooby and Shaggy run through your garden?
Squash!

N
NASTY CHARACTERS

What do you call a single vampire?
A bat-chelor.

What did the father ghost say to his son?
"Spook when you're spoken to!"

Which bank does a vampire visit?
The blood bank!

What did the bully have for lunch?
A knuckle sandwich!

What beverage can't a vampire drink?
SunnyD!

What do you call a dream where vam-pires are attacking?
A BITEmare!

Why didn't the skeleton go to the party?
He had no body to go with!

O
OSTRICHES & OTHER STRANGE ANIMALS

Why does an ostrich have such a long neck?
Because its head is so far from its body!

What do you get when you cross an elephant with a parrot?
An animal that tells you everything it remembers!

What do you give a sick bird?
Tweetment!

What kind of sick bird is against the law?
An ill-eagle.

What did the beaver say to the tree?
"It's been nice gnawing you!"

Why did the turkey cross the road?
It was the chicken's day off.

What animal has the highest intelligence?
A giraffe.

What do you say at the start of a turtle race?
"Ready, set, slow!"

P

PIRATES

What is a pirate's favorite restaurant?
Aaarrrby's.

Why are pirates pirates?
Because they aaarrr!

What is a pirate's favorite subject in school?
Aaarrr-t!

PRESTO CHANGE-O! (It's Magic!)

What did the ghost teacher say to his class?
"Look at the board, and I'll go through it again!"

Why didn't the penguin have any change in his pocket?
He put it in the snow bank!

What do you get if you cross a witch and an iceberg?
A cold spell!

What happened when the wizard and witch met?
It was love at first fright!

Q

QUEENS, KINGS & JOKERS

How do you wake a queen up?
Poker face!

Why did the king go to the dentist?
He needed a new crown.

What object is king of the classroom?
The ruler!

What do princes and books have in common?
Lots of pages!

What's the best part about living in a castle?
The knight life!

QUICK JOKES (The Shortest Jokes in the Book!)

Where do bunnies work?
I-Hop.

What bow can't you tie?
A rainbow!

What do chefs make with cars?
Traffic jam.

i ♥ Rainbows

R

SHAGGY'S REVENGE!
(Bad Jokes)

Why is 2+2=5 like your left foot?
It's not right.

What's the difference between a train and a teacher?
The teacher says, "Spit your gum out," and the train says, "choo-choo!"

Why did Shaggy eat his homework?
Because his teacher said it was a piece of cake.

RUH-ROH! (Truly Bad Jokes)

Where does Dogzilla park her car?
In the barking lot!

Why did the clock in the cafeteria always run slow?
Every lunch it went back four seconds!

Velma: We can't go swimming right now. We just ate, and you're not supposed to swim on a full stomach.
Shaggy: Like, that's okay, we'll swim on our backs.

S

SCOOBY'S FAVORITES

How can you tell a
dogwood tree?
By its bark.

What do you call
a dog sitting in
the snow drift?
A chili dog!

Where do you find a dog with no legs?
In a hotdog bun.

What do you call a good friend who sticks with you?
Scooby-Glue!

SHAGGY'S FAVORITES

Which letter is the coolest?
Iced T.

Why did Shaggy bring a ladder to the school assembly?
Because the music teacher told him to sing higher.

Teacher: How do you spell Mississippi?
Shaggy: Like, the state or the river?

What do you get when you cross Shaggy with a vampire?
A really ghoul dude!

SNACKS, SNACKS AND MORE SNACKS

Why does Shaggy drink so much hot chocolate?
Because he's a cocoa-nut!

What did the ghost order at the restaurant?
BOO-berry pie!

What did the baby ghost eat for dinner?
A BOO-loney sandwich!

Why did the boy blush when he opened the fridge?
He saw the salad dressing!

What does a ghost eat for breakfast?
Scream of Wheat!

Why are teddy bears never hungry?
Because they're always stuffed.

What do skeletons always order at a restaurant?
Spare ribs!

TELEPHONES, TEXT MESSAGES & TECHNOLOGY

How do skeletons call their friends?
On the tele-bone!

What do you call a computer superhero?
A screen saver.

Why did the computer sneeze?
It had a virus.

What do you get if you cross a goat with an elephant?
A ton of ram memory!

What did the mouse say to the webcam?
Cheese.

What do you get when you cross a computer with a vampire?
Something newfang-led!

How do trees get on the Internet?
They log in.

U

UNUSUAL BEHAVIOR

What do turtles wear in the winter?
Peopleneck sweaters.

How do you clean a tuba?
With a tuba toothpaste.

What did the fish say to his friend?
"Keep your mouth shut and you won't get caught!"

Why did the bear tiptoe past the campsite?
He didn't want to wake the sleeping bags.

What do you get if you cross an artist with a policeman?
A brush with the law!

What do you call a stuffed bear who won't come in from the cold?
A teddy brrrrrrrr.

What does a frog do when its car breaks down?
It gets toad.

V

VELMA'S FAVORITES

What do you do if a teacher rolls her eyes at you?
Pick them up and roll them back to her!

What does a novel wear when it's cold?
A book jacket.

What monsters are good at math?
None, unless you Count Dracula.

Why doesn't the sun go to college?
Because it has a million degrees!

Why did the Cyclops close his school?
Because he only had one pupil.

What did the math book say to the other math book?
"I've got problems."

How does a book about zombies begin?
With a dead-ication.

VENTRILOQUISTS &
OTHER DUMMIES

Knock Knock.
Who's there?
Nobody.
Nobody who?
Nobody here!

Knock Knock.
Who's there?
Dummy!
Dummy who?
Dummy a favor and go away!

VANS & OTHER SUPER GROOVY VEHICLES

Did you hear about the truck that delivered computers?
It crashed.

Why did the pioneers cross the country in covered wagons?
Because they didn't want to wait forty years for a train!

What do you call an angle that's been in a car crash?
A rectangle.

What's white, has a horn, and gives milk?
A dairy truck!

WIND & WEATHER

What did the tornado say to the hurricane?
"Wanna play Twister?"

Why do skeletons hate winter?
The cold goes right through them!

What did the tornado say to the sports car?
"Wanna go for a spin?"

What do you get when you cross a snowman and vampire?
Frostbite.

WHISPERS & SECRETS

Why is it against the rules to whisper?
Because it's not aloud!

Why is harder to keep secrets in the winter?
Because your teeth chatter when it's cold!

Why should you never tell a secret to a whale?
They're all blubber-mouths!

How did the Vikings tell each other secrets?
They used Norse code!

X

XYLOPHONES & OTHER WEIRD NOISES

How did the musician get locked out of his house?
All his keys were on the piano.

What do you call a car that sings?
A cartoon!

Why did the drummer bring a chicken to band practice?
He needed new drumsticks.

Why was the music teacher locked out of the classroom?
She had the wrong key.

X-RAYS & DOCTOR JOKES

Doctor, doctor, everyone says I'm invisible.
Who said that?

Doctor, doctor, I keep thinking there's two of me.
One at a time, please!

Doctor, doctor, I think I'm a spoon.
Sit over there, please, and don't stir!

Y YACHTS, BOATS & OTHER FLOATING THINGS

Where do boats go when they get sick?
To the dock.

What is the worst kind of vegetable to have on a yacht?
A leek.

Where is the best place for a station wagon to go swimming?
A car pool.

How does Scooby row a boat?
With a dog paddle!

YELLOW-BELLIED COWARDS

What's a coward's favorite desert?
I scream.

Why are all mummies cowards?
They never have any guts!

What day do chickens fear the most?
Fry-day!

Why was the egg scared?
He was a little chicken.

61

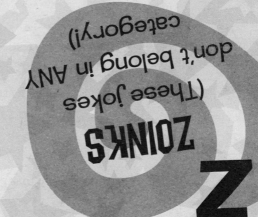

Z ZOINKS

(These jokes don't belong in ANY category!)

How do you keep a chicken in suspense?
I'll tell you later.

What do you call people who embarrass you in front of your friends?
Mom and Dad!

How do you calm a fire-breathing dragon?
Throw water on him so he'll let off some steam.

What music do they play at the Olympics?
Heavy medal.

What do you get from an Alaskan cow?
Cold cream!

What do you get when you cross a dog with a telephone?
A golden receiver.

Why is it hard to play games on the African savanna?
Because there are so many cheetahs!

Zoinks! Ruh-roh!
You just had the last laugh!